LOVES YOU

ALSO BY SARAH GAMBITO

Delivered
Matadora

LOVES YOU

Poems

Sarah Gambito

A Karen & Michael Braziller Book
PERSEA BOOKS / NEW YORK

Persea Books, Inc.
90 Broad Street
New York, NY 10004

Library of Congress Cataloging-in-Publication Data

Names: Gambito, Sarah Verdes, author.
Title: Loves you : poems / Sarah Gambito.
Description: New York : Persea Books, [2019] | "A Karen & Michael Braziller Book."
Identifiers: LCCN 2018041873 | ISBN 9780892554959 (original trade pbk. : acid-free paper)
Classification: LCC PS3607.A433 A6 2019 | DDC 811/.6—dc23
LC record available at https://lccn.loc.gov/2018041873

Book design and composition by Rita Lascaro
Typeset in Zapf Humanist

Manufactured in the United States of America. Printed on acid-free paper.

CONTENTS

What is patriotism but the love of the food one ate as a child.
—LIN YUTANG

LOVES YOU

On How to Use this Book

You deserve your beautiful life.

Its expectant icicles, the dread forest
that is not our forest.
And yet, we meet there.
The streams streaming through us.
The leaves leaving through us.

Once I was black-haired
and I sat in my country's lap.

I was so sure she was asking me
what I wanted.

Invite at least 15 people. It's okay if your apartment is small. Put 7 lb of cut up chicken in the biggest pot you own with 2 parts soy sauce 2 parts vinegar and 1 part water. Make sure to completely cover the chicken. Throw in a handful of black peppercorns, lots of bay leaves and two fistfuls of garlic cloves. Bring to a rolling boil and simmer until chicken is almost falling off the bone (around 45 minutes to 1 hour.) Place chicken on a baking sheet and broil for 10 minutes until the skin is crispy and slightly charred. Boil remaining liquid for 15–20 minutes to reduce and add 1 can coconut milk to make a sauce. Plate chicken and pour sauce over. Serve with so much white rice.

UMAMI

I Am Not From The Philippines

A white guy liked me and it was like
a lake might bend in half.

I wanted to go to The Olive Garden.
I said Yes with my eyes like platelets.

When God was Filipino,
he put a pig and fire together and called it porkissimo.

I grabbed a Filipino girl's hand and she said are you a lesbian.
I faked it to myself. I faked it to them all.

All the nurses ever, ever in the world
are Filipino.

Like a push in the gut, I rush past the hovels of hospital rooms.
The great digital of machines and humans simmering at work.

The pork chop of the leg poking from the blanket.
There will always be sick people. You'll always have a job.

Nurses with their white soft shoes. Their cuneiform writing.
The change purses of nurses diveting around.

My aunts mothers uncles cousins whiplashing into nurses.

Love Song

A young boy was shot to death so I wrote a poem and arranged it like salt around his vanished body. I said you can't go past here. Wind was flying in our faces.

I brought my friends with their leathery hands. Their hands like pylons and bread baskets and struggling rappers who sing baby, baby, baby.

How does it balance on crazy bird of paradise legs? The left hands of the clock aligning around a number cut to burgundy serifs.

How do we bear our own skin against ours? How we cooked for each other, told each other we were sick. We went to beaches and we were in pink bathing suits. Salty and fatty things were in the cooler and the belly of the sky was managed with stars.

Redeemer

()
I was
beachfront property on all sides.

()
I was holding your mustache. I was so cheap.
My people answered all your telephones.
We said hello??

()
The mouth is growing, the teeth are growing. Essentially, everything's
going to get gross in there.

()
YOU'LL DO WHAT THE WIVES WON'T DO, WON'T YOU?
DO YOU KNOW WHAT A BLUMPIE IS?

()
They pulled it out of the history books.
But, they couldn't pull the tooth roots out of the country.

()
The problem is your race is adolescent.

()
I'm 11 years old and wearing pin-striped jeans.
Someone yells
ME SO HORNY

()
I nebber heard such lies.

()
IS THAT YOUR SON?
Are you the nanny?

()
On the bus, Caroline calls someone a "fucker."
It is an insult? It means someone who fucks?
Someone believes the fucker is fuckable?

()
I am wearing pin-striped jeans
I am a message that I lie against.
I touch its soft ears.

()
WHY YOU DON'T LIKE ME? ARE YOU AFRAID OF A BIG DICK?

()
I was my life. It meant that I was hungry.
I was stopping myself in the streets and I said are you hungry.

()
What happened to your legs in this pond?
Everyone in heart-shaped inner tubes.

()
HELLO MY FRIEND I know you are not interested in me. But, I would
like to ask for your help. What is it, in general, that an Asian girl is
looking for? What is something that most Asian girls are attracted to?
Thank you for your help. Have a great day!

()
In my country, we didn't eat meat like you eat meat.
We ate vegetables and the juice from vegetables
Meat was like parmesan cheese.
Just sprinklings on top.

()
Blackguard against itself.
These girls shiver
with pleasure.

Cento

You laugh at your mollusk beating organs. You cover yourself with
your hands and you think. This is my skin not just the bag that keeps
everything together. I don't want to speak about race because it makes
you so angry. Organs bumping out like fishheads. When I bumped into
another Asian woman on the stairwell. We shouted. I'm sorry. I didn't
realize. How could you not realize when I'm standing here. I didn't
know if you were talking on your phone or going through your purse.
I'm not you. I'm not you. You are very weird. You are very weird.

Thunderdome

*After Emma realized that her white-collar job in the Philippines would
never pay her enough to send her children to college, she came to New York
and became a nanny.*
     —*The Cost of Caring,* The New Yorker, April 2016

I have this really vivid image of her on a bench in Central Park feeding
this white baby with a pink spoon. It was fall, and it was a bit chilly and
I thought to myself,
You Lost Your Mother.

—

The babies spank good. Brand spanking new.

It's like I just got used to the smell of her skin.

—

You know, the baby grew slim and tall like a clover.
She studied at the Sorbonne.
She made clothes for fashion shows,
for people covered in blue diamonds.

Surely you are rich over there

in the abroad.

It's not like here.

—

They *are* family. I love them. The oldest keeps asking me, do you really
love me? When I'm married, will you take care of my children?

—

I wanted my poem for us to suck on. Like an IV connected to the best ice tea in the world.

—

What is it to lie back in the best ice teas? The fronds of spearmint around you. A blanket of rice. A sparkler of oil in black pots. I knew you were cooking and that I could be big for my time. The bears of language would have no further alternative. We would fall into other's stews and aromatic dough. We would wash our hands together with sugar and salt and yellow flowers. Let's hand each other honeycomb with honeycomb in our hair.

I Like Chinese Food

That's my favorite kind. Indian food is too spicy so is Korean food. I really want to go Japan to eat sushi. I want to stand while they slit open all the fishes and I want to eat it right there on the platform. I changed my mind. I like Indian food but I would never cook it. Too many spices. Too much grating of vegetables. What is the difference between Thai holy basil and regular kind basil? It wouldn't be that big of a deal if I switched out one for the other? Do Filipinos eat dogs? They don't eat their own dogs, right? Just other people's? Or strays, I bet. Vietnamese food seems the healthiest out of all of them. Mostly veggies and broth.

We, Pacquiao

*"Later, I could not shake my suspicion that the shoulder brush, the whole
trip, was a dream. A vivid dream, of a place where every soul and everything
was lit from within by the still, small voice of Manny Pacquiao—Manny . . .
Emmanuel . . . Hebrew for 'God is with us'—but where Manny Pacquiao himself
was nowhere to be seen."*
    —*from "The Biggest Little Man in the World," GQ, April 2010*

We, Pacquiao, wear rubber masks and clean bathrooms. We cook
salisbury steak and wipe boogers off the ledges of gyms. We, as
Pacquiao, crowd around Pacquiao with our braised meats and gentle
Jewish savior. We bring you ice chips. We sew the in-lines of your work
pants. We contemplate the armpit energy of our sons and daughters
who grin and play dodge ball with mauve cardigans around their waists.
We, as Pacquiao, like a see-through foot we put in front of ourselves.
The foot shines unto itself and that is all. We are a black-haired god
sick with worry for us. His words We Pacquiao in big print. We speak
aloud in cancer wards in Chesapeake, under the sweet-skinned trees
of our childhood, over the coffin of a man whose name I remember as
Pacquiao. He was one of our flock and we were our shepherd.

Second Born

Her to the ends of my hair.

I'm aghast at the monolith cellulose of it. Needing things from me.

Frosted angel-shapes walking up and down escalators of good will.

And famished mouths below.

Can I tell you what I loved:

I was a child in the field of a church. Sweet gum and vetiver and danish. Buttercups littered the stage. I could run out into the octaves of buttercups and pick them—I and my children. A white girl held one up to my chin as our dresses fretted around us. She said look it's butter on you. I could only see if I did it to her. So we held it under our faces to see.

Cento

Do the food, wash the plates and glasses (especially the wine glasses!) by hand. Feed the dog and take him out to do Number 1 and Number 2. The floor does not get really clean if you use a mop. Go down to the hands and knees with the rag under the kitchen sink. Dilute the Mr. Klean with water so it lasts longer. Do the grocery. We like the pastured eggs. Everything else is not right. Do the laundry. Go take the dry cleaning. Drop the kids off at the bus stop. Then pick up the kids and drop them off at their after school activities. Pick them up at 4:00 pm and make sure they get afternoon snack. Chop fruit and veggies for their snack. Order the medications. Pick them up at the pharmacy. Wipe down the surfaces. If you can't find anything to do, come to me. You can always unmake beds and make them again. No fingernail polish, no lipstick, no cosmetics in general. No hairspray. No hair products other than shampoo. Wear the khaki pants I have set out for you. No skirts. All your shirts must cover your neck entirely, even in the summer. I like the mock turtlenecks. You can get these in short or long sleeved versions. Cut your hair short-short. A man's cut. It is like Sheena Easton. Don't stand in front of the air conditioner or any of the fans. This will blow your air into the house. You cannot cook Filipino food in the kitchen. You may not sit at the dining table or any of the chairs or sofas in the house. When you want to relax, please do this in your room. Don't address Mr. If there is anything you need, come to me. Wake up at 6:00 am and go to bed by 8:30 pm. We don't want to see the light from under your bedroom door. You have one day off. Please don't walk with your friends toward or around the house. You must bathe every night. Make sure you do this before 8:00 pm. Whenever you see anyone in the house, make sure you greet them. "Good morning!" or "Good afternoon!" or "Good evening!"

SOUR

Salmon Sinigang

My sister's favorite.

1 tablespoon olive oil
1 red onion, diced
5 garlic cloves, minced
1 teaspoon salt
4 tomatoes, cored and medium dice
1 cup dry white wine
1/2 inch piece fresh ginger (chopped)
3 cups water
Juice from 2 limes
3 tablespoons fish sauce
2 tablespoons white miso
1 pound salmon (cut into large cubes)
1 pound fresh green beans (trimmed)
Black pepper
Salt
Steamed white rice

1. Heat the oil over medium heat until shimmering. Add the onion, garlic, ginger and salt and cook, stirring occasionally, until softened, about 5 minutes. Add the tomatoes and sauté around 5 minutes.

2. Add the wine and scrape up any browned bits from the bottom of the pot, and bring to a boil. Reduce the heat to medium low and simmer until the wine is reduced by about half, about 7 minutes.

3. Add the water, lime juice, fish sauce and stir to combine. Return to a simmer and cover with a tightfitting lid. Simmer about 5 minutes.

4. Ladle about 1/2 cup of the liquid into a small bowl, add the miso, and stir until completely dissolved. Add the miso mixture back to the pot and stir to combine.

5. Increase the heat to medium, add the salmon and green beans and stir to combine. Simmer until salmon has cooked and the green beans have softened, about 3 minutes. Taste and season with additional salt and or lime juice as needed. Serve with steamed rice.

Adapted from Marvin Gapultos

Protection

We were refugees against the usual things. I scattered baby teeth around the perimeter. Things like bruschetta confused me. I picked up rastering body parts and I blew them out like bubbles, like store signs. I existed in the ear canals of the stacked cities. Many bells sounding at the same time opened up to Americans standing on scales. Holding their skin in calipers. I loved Jesus so much. I rubbed and rubbed until my bracelets fell off of me.

Cento

I was the young girl with moon lipstick
on the scooter
I was breaking eggs everywhere.

I yelled NA SA REALI KO
because I saw it in movies
and it was my mother tongue.

I made a cookbook for my mothers.
I couldn't see the date and then I could.
It meant that I was seventeen
and I was trying to cook for everyone.

I said rich-mond
because I was new to this country.
I picked up a melon and I was confused
because I said to it Asian faces.
I said he's dead and there is no justice
and I get that there maybe never can be
but there is a lot of anger.

And I threw the melon.

I was finishing a tedious task.
I was correcting grammar
or weaving a shawl
or peeling a thousand parsnips.

Because I could.
Because my life could depend on it.
I was dancing by myself on the dance floor
with the remnants of my work
around me and everyone even
my one beloved family was gone.

I said look you are at the center of it and I
traced the center spindle of the dancing floor.
But I was alone.

What hurt most was that my mother
was in the car and I thought that she
was going to leave me but I wasn't sure.
I saw the small likeness of a mother
floating in a river.
I heard my sister say
on the phone it's not right how they did that.
Her voice breaking into fingerprints.

My Palate was Snub like a Goat's Nose

I pushed it into bags that crinkled
with indestructible muffins.
We lived in the plastic foliage
of the great malls of the city.
Watching and laughing preemptively
in case someone points out WHO IS THAT?
We sidled up to the great breasts of the southern churches.
We sang with our shaven underarms
and our black-haired children like loose change.
Our difficult jobs clucking like chickens.

I don't care about the inert mint of the myth.
The glass citizenship of the myth.
The myth with its SSL and irritated house guest.
The blanket I yanked off of you this morning.

Citizenship

I was so afraid. I couldn't escape it. It was bigger than me and three-
horned. It dashed for me and missed and missed again. It leapt for me
in my skirt. I was younger than it. It opened its parent mouth and I
could die trying to figure it out.

It would never never miss me.
It would stand on its two legs,
and I was its message.

I'm still surprised by our unsugared silhouette.

Our hopeful investments and slightly whiny children.

Pompous jars of mustard in the fridge.

Us, as blunt as gum

under tables in restaurants.

Immigration

My sister said I better get a job with this nursing thing. What kind of person doesn't get a job after going to school for something like this. She became a mother several times. She smiled and I saw the new moon of the smiles of her children. They were kind and solicitous and gathering at the base of our reunion. A law flew down the river's currents and our crops drank the law and we were in pots of ourselves.

She wrote her name like a poem and there was a division symbol and the pots of her name and it was *kaakit-akit* healing. She said, tell me about poetry. I really want to know. It meant that she really wanted to know me. I took that as a truth and I crossed myself on Jesus and Jesus because he brought us to this place with its chicken restaurants and beef restaurants and pig restaurants.

Holiday

Crashing across cousin stars with deep listening holes. Because we're related and every wren that has nested abroad would like to become my mother. I'd like to lie flayed open upon her twelve breaking torsos. This blood would weld us to the chair and I'd let a crowd in. I'd always thought that crowds were created in a panic. A great anti-system of people fleeing fire. Rather, crowd dynamic is cultivated because you run towards. You want concert tickets or something to do the day after thanksgiving. They're almost giving it away. This is what she says as the gold metal hits the outline of her. She says I want you to find me. I want that you never give up and you find me.

When I Hated My Body

The elders gathered from the cornices of the island's arms and we had nothing to say. Even hedge funds with the power to hoover it up and offer it back like tightly packed cigarettes were silent.

When you were a child, your eyelashes were so long.
We used to call you pilik mata.

I almost posted this on "social media"

You eat like you are being chased.

You who are living. What is your responsibility?

Illuminated light and

holding the hymnal with your boyfriend,

I wanted the poems to breathe prettily,

to be ecstatic and extroverted citizens.

SALT

One Night Only

The recipe invites itself to eat and laughs at its own jokes.
Puns of tripled and quadruped meanings.
Was I ratting on you?
I invite everyone. Everyone is my friend.
Would you like some of my sandwich?
I really mean you can come forward
with your mouth open.
Once, I wrote a play. There was only one scene.
A girl lists the food she wants to eat.
Jasmine rice sauteed in garlic and sesame oil. A fish you caught yourself.
I put gold flecks in the sauce so everyone will know how happy we are.
I call the play *Loves You Long Time*.
The manuscripts are drying and dying out in mouldering museums.

Pick one:

1. Filipinos don't care about their history.
2. Filipinos can't afford to preserve the manuscripts in this kind of
   tropical heat.
3. Los manuscripts no existe. I only told you about them because I
   love you and you love me.

Arroz Caldo

My father would make this on post-holiday days when we had to feed a lot of people and quickly. This was my day-after-Christmas. My day-after-New Years.

4 tablespoons olive oil
One 1-inch piece of ginger root, finely chopped
1 onion, chopped
8 minced cloves garlic
1 pound boneless, skinless chicken
2 tablespoons fish sauce
1 cup short grain rice
4 cups chicken broth
Green onions, thinly sliced, as garnish
Fried garlic flakes
Lime juice from 2 limes

Heat oil in a large pot or Dutch oven over medium heat. Add the ginger, onion, and garlic and cook until the onion is translucent.

Add the chicken and cook until browned, about 5 minutes. Add the fish sauce and simmer for a few minutes, then add rice and simmer a few minutes more, stirring often. Add the chicken broth and bring to a boil. Lower heat and let simmer, stirring frequently until the chicken and rice are cooked through, about 25 to 30 minutes.

Heat a few tablespoons of oil in a skillet over medium-high heat. Add the remaining 3 cloves of minced garlic and fry until a deep golden brown. Transfer the flakes to a paper towel and set aside.

Add lime juice. Sprinkle with fried garlic flakes and green onions.

Cento

I

My country untangles its horns
and licks its own agave.

II

We might meet at a table with fresh grapes,
with the top of my head overflowing.
We speak of quiet things and these things
quiet me all the long silver way.
We walk in our own gardens which could be a shared garden.

III

To be in love and to accept so little of the world.
I knew that someone might govern the mailroom moon.

IV

A teacher once told me to beware
of the first person.
The little girl voice.

V

My hair would be sea-green and I would write my myth
in squid ink. It would be inscrutable and mine only
and therefore irrefutable.

VI

I drink cacao with my country.

VII

We are enterprising
in our horsehair embroidered costumes.

VIII
I said, what about the MacArthur Memorial
in Virginia, the MacArthur Suite in Manila?
She said that this was under reconstruction.
She was pissed at me for some reason.

IX
I made no effort to control my American accent.
I knew that it would humiliate her. Or, perhaps that is my fantasy.

X
The many legs, the fathom legs. My country in many countries
in my dialects and flower flecked vocabularies
named for a Spanish king who never visited.

XI
Did King Philip II of Spain visit the Philippines,
the country conquered by his country
and named after him during his lifetime?

XII
Answer
Yes.
And he said that this is a very GOOD country for me to live at.

XIII
Some tourists said that they wanted to return to the Philippines
to have a vacation again; while others wanted to live here!
It depends if you like tropical places.
Plus, there's a huge mall in the Philippines and lots of Pretty Beaches.

First Born

I want the outer R of the poem to be wintergreen.
the smell of homemade Play-Doh, of toothpaste.
Something available in drugstores.
I want to catch my hand in my face.
To read a poem from a decade ago
as if you were that girl.
Urgent like a fig over a pelvis.
I want to peel the natal paper away from a baby.
The island crocus. The wary gorilla.
All those muscles just from eating berries!
I can't barely handle all the dials and switches on myself.
What more on a bright-eyed chip-eating creature that says "mudder."
I hunt my mother like a mother.
A jazzy assemblage of roast potatoes
clumps of protein and sugar
like rusty scuba gear.
Basically: my wish is that you are never, never pierced through the heart.
My aim is ordinary.
My anthem open. My berries gasping together in pie.

Yolanda: A Typhoon

How much our hands are God's
to be running fingers over braille cities.
We are this hand pushed through our womb.
Weeping with each other's blood in our eyes.
I dreamed that I slept with the light on.
I was asleep in my mother's bed because my father was out to sea
Sweet, small fishing rod. Ears of wind rushing through many jellied trees.
We were on this cardboard earth with its puffing volcanoes,
miniature baseball players and horrible winds
scored by musician's hands.
Stand in the strong ear of this love.

Asado

I smile so hard and trees

drop in my native country.

When my aunties were mopping the public restrooms,
I thought one day, one day I'll get to do that.

My family picks its teeth and watches game shows.
She has no use for me.

You're so nice. You're so nice.
That's what she said when I worked at a store folding panties.

It was my *job* to be nice.
I'm making you believe that I'm running next to you.

Adjusting the hair out of their eyes

as our sun bullrushes into our faces.

Bilingual

I pull down her hair
wiping the Lord
with strawberry scent.

I'm here to feed these
that pass through
the free museums.

Our crystal
bowls of pasta
on the v-counter.

I want you to hear
the fingertips of a language
that is not yours,
the shampooed heads
of women I am not.

A strong and velcro shrub.
A gorgeous alien
with a thousand headed eyes.

What our ancestor
is frightened of blacklights
into a million fisted flower
and we push my face deep in earth.
Deer stop moving
to admire
our days
kneeling before me.

Without so disassembling,
I disassembled.

Fresh under the rain
I hold my body in its
brown basket.

The wires
and trades of the body
fragrant and ever-seeing.

She said the rain made her hair come down
in points that met each other.
The rain becomes a metaphor
rather than just what happens.
You should want to tell a story.
But, I want more, more than *that*.

Take Your Time

25 cloves of garlic
6 tablespoons extra-virgin olive oil
1 28-ounce can crushed San Manzano tomatoes
1 teaspoon hot red-pepper flakes
1/2 teaspoon salt
1/2 teaspoon sugar
1 lb cooked pasta
Pecorino cheese

Cook garlic in oil in a small heavy pot over low-medium heat, stirring occasionally, until golden, 3 to 5 minutes. Add tomatoes, red-pepper flakes, salt and sugar and simmer, stirring occasionally, for 1 hour. Add to 1 pound of pasta. Sprinkle heavily with pecorino.

Old Dominion

When I was born,
the woman ahead of me
had a lovely Om and it was
an Apostle. Children sang around
me and I sang Edelweiss, Nothing but
the Blood and come cookie stick.

In my church, I petted
my spine. I was furry
and luxuriant. Grass growing
nearer. I stood among my conifers
and when no one was
looking I played every character
in the Nativity. I liked it
best when I was Mary
freezing at night.
I kissed the top of
my dollbaby's head while
cars peeled in fleur de lis
around me.

My church
was tall and level-headed.
My church memorized
scripture and made peachy
fingernails and emotional
outbursts in school.

Sundays

We go to D.C. to look at the stately tudor houses
and imagine the breakfasts in there.
The children with their toys with expensive knobs.
We laugh in our shaggy car.
We love the gleaming foreheads of those houses.
We power back to our little potluck in the red trees.
Tita Marie handing out pork barbecue like scepters.
Kool-aid, KFC on paper plates.

Barbecue Scepters

2 lb pork shoulder, sliced in inch cubes
Bamboo skewers

For marinade:

3 tsp minced garlic
1/2 cup soy sauce
1/4 cup lemon juice
1/2 cup ketchup
1 can ginger ale
1/2 cup brown sugar
1/4 tsp red pepper flakes
1 tsp salt
1 tsp pepper

Mix the marinade ingredients in a large bowl. Reserve ½ cup of the marinade. Pour the rest of the marinade over the pork and refrigerate overnight.

Skewer the pork pieces on the bamboo sticks. Heat grill to medium high. Brush reserved marinade onto skewers and grill around 8–10 minutes on each side until slightly charred.

BITTER

Sundays

1 bitter melon, seeds and insides removed and cut into thin slices
4 tablespoons white wine vinegar
2 medium tomatoes diced
2 eggs beaten slightly
1 tablespoon minced garlic
1 medium-sized onion sliced
Salt and pepper
Chopped parsley
3 tablespoons olive oil

Place the bitter melon in a large bowl and sprinkle liberally with salt. Add white wine vinegar and let stand for six minutes. In a large pan, sauté the garlic and onions in oil until the garlic is golden brown and the onions are translucent. Add the tomatoes and cook until soft. Add the bitter melon and cook for 4 minutes. Pour the eggs over the mixture and stir until eggs are done and bitter melon is tender. Season with salt and pepper. Garnish with parsley and serve with white rice.

Duty

My father would come back in the still dead of the night and eat eggs—one after another—while my mother watched in silence. What do you say to someone who has been gone for that long? Newspapers collecting on the front lawn. Squabbles left unopened like easter foil chocolates. My sister and I found these badly. Slower than the other children. Afraid we didn't understand English well. OK. Go, now. OK. Now you can go.

My sister was sweet and followed me doing things. She had a doll with wondrous skin. The doll was careful like a honeysuckle and artless like a honeysuckle. I liked to hold her near. She was closemouthed and did not cry and it pleased me immensely and I was ashamed to be pleased. Children should never be quiet. Like the quiet daughters we were. We quiet. Our crayons. Quiet.

Holiday

I want to lick someone
with an antelope for a head.
A whole-person-boxer for a fist.
Circulatory, fruited over
nostalgia to overcome me like
a truck I'll drive over his body
while he reaches for a
telephonic hip. The way gods
do when they create
the first animal cracker
steams of existence.
Fat plant and vernix.
The shattered cursive equations
my love was capable of.
I said there will never be a night like this.
How is it I was right?
How fibrous and incidental it seems.
The tiny leather jackets we wore.
What was it about that quality that I admired?
Loping around like a christening polecat.

Baby Alive

To turn the dollar on its container,
we are lucky to see behind the pepperoni "its" of the doll.
Its race.
The associative élan of the doll the person wanted to be.
Our legs were cold and so we fought over the towel
and could not, did not rest.
I'm excited to tell you about my baby only I've gained 30 lbs
and I'm afraid you'll only be looking at the fat on my arms and ass.
The doll could poop if you spoon a gelatinous matter in its mouth.
There was powder to mix with water to make this so.
Of course, the doll was real to any girl
who saw the amorous commercials
of the doll's deliciously flaccid limbs.
We envy the utter sleep of the invalid, the baby, the unalive.
I wish I could protect you from anyone who does not see you as I do.
I've laid your limbs out like so.
You'll move them.
Maybe you will.
Maybe you won't.

hapa

flush against the sycamore
of blood type, increased risk
or immunity for specific diseases,
or the thousands of basic biochemical
ways I painted my nails gold
I said, who would be dunked
into that code of a polypeptide or an RNA chain
like a pearl without eyes
like a son with blue eyes
pushing the soul through bicycle spokes
it spoke with a vibrato
that embarrassed me
a function in the organism
orangutan nanny in the garage
my pleasure—a disappointment
a golden wig
myself singing to the vulva of the sky
that denotes a part or fragment of something,
your child who I choose
to love like a dreadnaught
a sailor with braids on his body
lonely for us both

Unbabies

()
My son brushed and brushed his teeth and there was blood. He said can my gums be pink like white people?

()
There's a story about another son who was unruly and uneducated and handsome in all the lagoons. This son died and the parents walked all over the cities and mountains and nothing would help. No one tells you that you can't even write about it. The emblems close all their mouths. There is no pert inner life. No bite-size gem.

()
There was still another son who was young and getting married. He had 6 different wedding suits all alive with pearls. The fanning fanned out behind him. He was supposed to go out to someone much loved and there were so many vegetables to marvel at and cook with in commodious planters on sills.

()
I grow hair over these dark sons. I hide them all—my un-babies. Sons that cannot walk the street safely. When my son was born, the first thing he said was "peeeesh" with his fingers like a gun. He said he was going to Guam. He "vacationed" there but grew up here and couldn't afford it. He was an artist, a painter of war scenes. I said his name like puffs of cumulus on an unhurt day. I was a poet when I loved him. I woke with the fingers of my heart in second gear.

Advice

In the sinkhole of the house

the lost breastplate

I gathered my coupons

I held my face over the face

of my daughter

I saw the foal-barn where

we lay down on scraps

mouthed "shekel" and "beast"

I was large unto my barn

and she looked back from the prow of my ill-ease

if I drop her

if I drop her (and catch her)

nonetheless—

she falls (would have fallen)

so I crouch close to the egg of the lee of this stone

that finds its mark because its warrior is keen and female and long ago
I took all our own battery operated ponies with the boarish manes that
pinged as my fingers traveled over them. Warriors with suns on their
backs that held the horses that foamed and birthed and broke in my
hands.

Why is it I haven't done anything

and yet I want so much to drape it around someone's shoulders

SWEET

Bibingkang Malakit

2 cups glutinous sweet rice
4 cups coconut milk
1 1/2 cup brown sugar
1/2 tsp salt
3/4 cup coconut cream

Bring coconut milk to boil in a large skillet. Add rice and salt and
cook on medium heat. Stir constantly, as if you are making a risotto,
until rice is tender and almost dry, about 15 to 20 minutes. Stir in 3/4
cup brown sugar, lower heat and cook, covered, 5 minutes. Spread
cooked rice mixture in a greased foil lined 8" square pan. Combine
the remaining sugar and the thick coconut milk. Pour on top of rice in
pan and spread evenly. Broil in oven for 4 to 5 minutes or until top is
brown. You're going to have a very certain regard for the people that
you make this for as the rice gets very heavy as it cooks and you cannot
stop stirring. I first made this in summer for Joseph and Kron and I did
not realize how long I would need to stand in front of a hot oven.

Marriage

Just as tasting ice cream,
the outer mouth-rim of aluminum of what enjoys us.
Blades of grass at a sudden still.
The exclamations of money and mercy done
and I'd like to live with you suspended above the superdome.
Why should we not have beautiful earrings?
Trying to see plosions of wild thyme in summer grass,
I fell asleep next to you.
Or, I was stirring pots of wonderful things next to you.

Virginia

I smell vanilla like an ability. It fills my new houses and I admit people
into these houses. The people are jealous and squat or full of picnics.
Every window has a view of the sea and I love the sea. I wear a yellow
dress and someone says that is just like Hamlet. Someone else says.
You are so right. It is just like Hamlet. Only it never is. It's just people
posing next to each other. Their stretch marks eeking out like kings.
The dirty whimpering pets. The flashdance costumes. Here we all are—
winking at the camera.

Sundays

Nothing can replace when we sat at the wood table.
Another country's light bat-shy
around our heads,
which nod to each other.

We hold smooth shapes of
immigrant coolnesses and hotnesses.

Can't we be here without trying to make it crescendo.
Can't it declare itself—a spell for itself.
A family reading in different rooms.

I'm tired of holding up pictures of the bodies.

I made copies
in case you want to see.

For it to be ineluctable.
Barely a good and grasped hand.

To admit that I didn't die,
I would like to hold all these branches in my mouth.
To unconnect the beatific animal
that has everything on cassette.

How do you live?
As obdurate as limestone,
of a celadon vase,
of cool bowls of things to delight you.

I wanted it to be a set of rubbery instructions
that would enable you to rub the tousled heads of pets.
Their finite happinesses.

Integers with gleaming scales,
the unpanicked ending to a okay story.

First on scene.
Mise en scene.
Mise en place.

Watermelon Agua Fresca (For When You Need Me)

15 cups chopped seedless watermelon (one 10-pound melon)
1 quart pink grapefruit juice
1/2 cup chopped mint
1/4 cup lime juice
1 quart ginger ale
1 bottle white wine
Ice

Purée watermelon in a blender until smooth. Pour into a large bowl and let stand for 15 minutes. Skim foam from surface and discard. Set a fine-mesh sieve over a large pitcher and strain purée into pitcher. Stir in grapefruit juice, ginger ale, mint, lime juice and white wine.

Serve in ice-filled glasses and know how much I love you.

Sundays

We would go to flea markets and my grandfather would say to people

sitting squashed in their lawn chairs.

I'll give you one dollar for dat.

The people would say NO. The detritus of their lives spread out like cat litter on folding tables.

My grandfather would ask again

I'll give you one dollar for dat.

I'd round and round looking at earrings I knew no one would buy me.

My hair was short like a pool boy's.

I wanted falcon feathers for earrings.

On display: broken shoes and plates with children in Dutch costumes painted on them. Belts of every size and books with people pulling at each other's lapels and duck dusters. Small watches with the crystals bashed in and paintings with mountains and sunning horses and sometimes someone would say YES.

Cento: Don't Eat Filipinos!

Filipino's perfect combination of real chocolate and crunchy biscuit creates
their delightful taste and texture. They're three delicious flavors available: white
chocolate, black chocolate and milk chocolate.
    —Nabisco Iberia

On August 26, 1999 then Philippine president Joseph Estrada called
the brand "an insult." So the government of the Philippines filed a
diplomatic protest with the government of Spain and the European
Commission.

I like it because it means that we are small and cute and sweet.

Former foreign Secretary Domingo Siazon reportedly said "he saw
nothing wrong with the use of 'Filipinos' as a brand name for the
cookies, noting Austrians do not complain that small sausages are
called Vienna sausages."

Do citizens of Berlin get upset that they gave the name to the Berliner
pastry? What about the Danish and the Danish Pastry? Or Cubans?

Actually, they taste pretty good!

Filipinos are produced by Artiach, a Spanish brand that is part of the
UK's United Biscuit. Its website claims that Filipinos are the leading
chocolate biscuit in Spain.

The Spaniards Christianized the Filipinos which is a good thing.
However, education to the masses, government, modernity and
technology was introduced by the Americans. Thus, I think the
Philippines is much better during the American colonization.

Mi favorito es aplastado Filipinos en gelato de vanilla.

Attaching the name Filipinos to a sweet product with a hole in the middle that is consumed for pleasure and contains little nutritional value is not very charming.

My Husband's Lychee Macarons

Instead of eating Filipinos, make these and enjoy. My husband makes these for our annual Christmas party.

When I make macarons, I make macarons. Since I only do this once a year, I go all in. It's an all day affair, like 12–14 hours. I have 4 baking sheets, with matching silicone mats. The biggest bottleneck is waiting for the cookies to set, and then waiting for them to cool so you can take them off the mats and reuse for the next batch. Tailor your recipe to your level of commitment. The buttercream recipe typically makes enough for multiple batches (5–7 batches of 24 cookies), which I usually infuse with multiple flavors: lychee, pistachio, raspberry, blueberry, etc. The favorite is lychee. The buttercream will refrigerate (good for around 3 days) or even keep in the freezer for a decent amount of time. I do recommend making a day of it. These are extraordinarily temperamental. It may take many batches for you to fine-tune your technique.

Macaron Shells

Ingredients (single batch of cookies)

3 egg whites (let warm to room temp or place in warm water for 5 min for quick fix)
1/4 cup white sugar
1 2/3 cups confectioners sugar
1 cup almond flour (finely ground)
1 pinch of cream of tartar
Powdered food coloring of your choice (works better than liquid)

Directions

1. Line 2 baking sheets with silicone baking mats

2. Sift almond flour in fine mesh strainer (use tablespoon to press through the strainer), separating out under-processed almond pieces, leaving only the fine flour. This will make your cookie shell surfaces smooth. Repeat process for the confectioner's sugar. Mix thoroughly with a fork in the same large bowl

3. Making the meringue. Beat egg whites in a bowl with a mixer on medium to high until the whites are foamy and glistening (roughly 30 seconds). Add pinch of cream of tartar (helps stabilize egg whites, generally making it more fool-proof). Beat in white sugar and continue beating until egg whites are glossy, fluffy and hold soft peaks (roughly 60 seconds)

4. Mix in powdered food coloring to egg whites gently, but quickly to desired hue (overcolor, as it fades during baking). Don't overmix, as you don't want to ruin your meringue. The powder stains, and a little goes a long way, so be careful.

5. Fold egg white mixture into almond flour-confectioners mixture until completely integrated using a rubber spatula. Roughly about 30 strokes. Should feel like mixing "molten lava" when done

6. Spoon mixture into a plastic Ziploc bag. The easy way to do this is put the Ziploc sandwich bag inside a glass, with the top of the bag folded over the glass. Using the rubber spatula, spoon it into the bag. Once it's all in, pull the bag out, and zip it up. Cut a small piece of the corner of the bag off (roughly 3/8 of an inch equilateral triangle). Using the bag, pipe a cookie shell about 1 1/4 inch in diameter in a corkscrew/circular pattern starting on the outside and finishing the piping in the middle of the cookie. The cookies will spread out due to gravity (depending on the consistency of the batter); as such, don't overfill or place too close together. Should be able to fit roughly 24 cookies per baking mat.

7. Once all the cookies have been piped onto the baking mats, bang the baking sheet onto a hard flat surface 2–3 times to help release air trapped inside the cookie shells. Repeat as necessary; though expect diminishing returns after the first two rounds. Using a fork tine, gently pop any large bubbles on the surface, to minimize distortion to the cookie surface

8. Let them rest at least 40 minutes. This will allow the surface to harden, leaving the base as the easier source of growth during baking. This is the secret to good macaron "feet."

9. Preheat oven to 285°F

10. Bake cookies until set, but not browned. I usually cook 7 min, rotate, cook an additional 7 minutes, but oven temps vary. Bake 1 tray at a time

11. Let cool completely

Buttercream

Ingredients (this will make at least 5–6 batches of cookie filling. Modify as desired)

2 1/2 cups sugar
10 large egg whites
4 cups (8 sticks or 2 pounds) of unsalted butter. Cut into pieces (roughly the size of a starburst candy)
2 teaspoons pure vanilla extract

Directions

1. Place sugar and egg whites in heat proof bowl. Set the bowl over a pot of gently simmering water, whisking in the sugar until dissolved and the egg whites are not too hot to touch (roughly about 3 minutes). Rub the mixture between your fingers, as it should feel completely smooth when ready.

2. Using a mixer, beat on high until it has cooled and formed stiff glossy peaks, roughly 10 min.

3. Add the butter, one piece at a time until incorporated. Repeat until all added. Don't worry if it looks curdled, it will become smooth again with continued beating. Add vanilla, and beat until just combined.

4. Turn mixer to lowest speed to eliminate air pockets. Roughly 5 minutes

5. Set aside enough to fit in a normal-sized Ziploc sandwich bag (roughly 2–3 cups)

Lychee Flavoring

1. Wash and then peel the skin off 20–30 lychees.

2. Using a paring knife, remove the fruit from the pit. I would recommend doing this over a large bowl to salvage all the juice you can.

3. Once the fruit has been separated, using a fine mesh strainer, force the fruit through the strainer with the back of a metal spoon. Save the juice, discard the pulp inside the strainer. If the fruit is too tough, one might blend it first, then force it all through the strainer

4. Now the "fun" part, emulsifying the juice into the apportioned buttercream. I apologize in advance. Using a fork, keep mixing the juice into the buttercream until fully integrated. It may seem a Sisyphean task, but it will eventually emulsify. I promise.

Finishing Macarons

1. Gently separate the cookies from the silicone baking mats. If undercooked, they will be sticky (modify next time based on your oven). If the inside of the cookie has flattened leaving a shell but nothing of substance underneath, you either underwhipped or overwhipped your meringue (adjust accordingly for next batch).

2. Match similar size cookies together so top matches bottom size wise

3. Pipe lychee buttercream roughly the same height as the "feet," though at your discretion.

4. Gently place the top shell onto buttercream, rotating/twisting to give a nice tight fit

5. Refrigerate for at least 4 hours (I'd recommend 24 hrs). The buttercream will soften up the inside of the shells, making them even more delectable.

6. Pick your theme song to have playing when you surprise your guests with one of the most difficult things you'll ever make. Recommendations: Archers of Loaf, Web In Front; Beastie Boys, Shadrach; Black Moon, Who Got Props?; David Bowie, Rebel Rebel; Destroyer, Dream Lover; Dr. Dre, Wit Dre Day (And Everybody's Celebratin'); The Doors, Peace Frog; Edwin Starr, Twenty-Five Miles; Ghostface Killah, Rec-Room Therapy; Le Tigre, Deceptacon; Madonna, Get Into The Groove; Marvin, This Loves Starved Heart Of Mine (It's Killing Me); The Misfits, Astro Zombies; The National, All The Wine; New Order, Age Of Consent; B.I.G, Juicy; Outkast, B.O.B; Prince, 1999; Shannon, Let The Music Play; Shout Out Louds, Hard Rain; The Smiths, Barbarism Begins At Home; Smokey, More Love; Stereolab, Les Yper-Sound; Tribe, Oh My God (Remix); Zeppelin, Immigrant Song

Ancestor

The one woven into brass tapestry. Heavy with rain
where weak neck babies cry from a sideways newspaper. Flashlight
when you shine through, the veins of our house fill with maples.
I traveled with my small cloudy hands.
I drank wine out of plastic cups.

You can't depend on the trapeze of your ears.
The poor warthogs of your hands.
You hold them pingponging in your hands.
Your hands in hands of everybody in different churches.

How beautiful to be gusted in these different ways.
Glassine and shaking yourself with canine aplomb.
He had the immigrant captain kirk way of speaking.

I want you to be deeply heard.
For you to take for granted that people
will hear what you say.
But, for you not to be naive or surprised
when people turn away.

When I was brave, I pushed my feet into the pedals
and these pushed me into the world I wanted to be in.
I was high and above all the other birds.
The birds flew in harlequins around me.

How to Turn Water into Wine

The daughters are coughing and stretching and reading books about themselves. I wrote these books. I held them in the palm of my hand like scallops, like gold clips in my hair when we saw my breath on the steppes. We repeated each other, you and I. I saw your handwriting, your cloth-covered books. We touched each other's mouths as mothers.

Where is the poem where blood pushed through the fabric?

Real as strawberries. Broke as hell to the touch.

The daughters grow old and I see the wood of their lives through their jowls. I hunker down in the corner and I care about them. The dead plants they pull with their fingers. Their store-bought hair and foreign, non-sequitur way of speech.

ACKNOWLEDGMENTS

Grateful acknowledgment goes to the following publications, in which some of these poems first appeared:

American Poetry Review, Black Clock, Ciamarron Review, Cream City Review, Colorado Review, Crazyhorse, Denver Quarterly, Drunken Boat, Field Magazine, Harvard Review, jubilat, Massachusetts Review, The Normal School, Poetry, Texas Review, Salt Hill and *Tin House.*

Thank you, as always, to Gabriel Fried for believing. Hearty thanks also to Michael and Karen Braziller for making a home for this book.

For Kundiman. More cornucopia.

I'm grateful to Fordham University and my colleagues in the English Department and in the Creative Writing Program.

To my NYC Barkada: Ricco Siasoco, Lara Stapleton, Marissa Aroy, Gina Apostal, Hossannah Asuncion, Nita Noveno, Ligaya Mishan, J. Mae Barizo, Leslie Norton, Nancy Bulalacao and Jessica Hagedorn.

For Rebecca Gambito, Carlito Gambito, Christine and Steve Rodgers, Joseph O. Legaspi, Vikas Menon, David Rolfing, Pavneet Singh, Tan Lin, Charlotte Meehan, Aimee Nezhukumatathil, Celia Quinn, Jennifer Chang, Deb Paredez, Eddie del Rosario, Pam Pickens, Marc Reinerth, Marilyn Rifkin, Oliver de la Paz, Patrick Rosal, Jon Pineda, Cathy Linh Che, Emily Dalton, Heather Bryant, Karen Pittleman, Rita Zilberman, Kron Vollmer, Marie Sarmiento, Jennifer Madriaga, Beth Frost, Myung Mi Kim, Kimiko Hahn, Roohi Choudhry, Henry W. Leung, Matthew Olzmann, Hyejung Kook, James Kim, Samiya Bashir, Timothy Yu, Carolyn Micklem, Stacey Robinson, Cave Canem and CantoMundo.

Most of all, this book is for John and Justin. You are the hibiscus heart. You are the dream.

Brave, Brave, Brave

Remember when we were so angry
and the presents were just empty
boxes wrapped in fancy paper?
We wore choir robes and faced
the choirmaster who was old and brown and soprano.
She said, "I want more than singing.
Cradle me in this song."
We knew instantly what she wanted.
Let's try now.

Cradle me in this song.

I weep in the pew because I want to cradle you
and I want to be cradled.
I weep now writing this to you.
I see the scrollwork of the song we are writing.

What if I was an ordinary person.
And I loved
only you.

And I moved over the bay, over the inlet, over the lake,
over the sea to be with you under the eaves.

Empire

I'd grab hold of an elbow belonging to an animal possessed of a
precious substance. Delicate dolls used to be carved from the stuff.
But can no longer now. You say this as the dolls lounge on your hand.
You say can no longer now. We're at a party that we want to succeed.
I'm the ringer and I say ooooo. Once there was a girl that looked
like me. She had a spectacular mustache and I was sure I was like a
female Prince & the Revolution. The whites of their eyes, dripping hair,
fulsome clothes and vining guitar. How did I hold the fruit plant inside
of us without crushing it? The young girl with the fact of her body. Face
still not limber enough for certain emotions. Pool depth. Laughing
underwater.

The New Child

She says I am going to be a Pop Star
and she has these antelope
banging
from a grenadine hatchback.
Girls with eyes rimmed with sumac
and drugstore gold dust
razoring sideways through the pig factories.
Who fills time up like a paper bag for no reason?
Who builds these cartilage walls of slum,
of chalcedony while
God pushes my belly forward?
You atheists sit in your sterilized atom
while I bling these zirconias.
How do you know what I'm rocking isn't real?
I rock this shit in the public schools of the world.